The Earth-Owl
and other moon-people

FOR

FRIEDA AND NICHOLAS

THE EARTH-OWL

and other moon-people

by

TED HUGHES

illustrated by

R. A. BRANDT

FABER AND FABER

24 Russell Square

London

First published in mcmlxiii
by Faber and Faber Limited
24 Russell Square London W.C.1
Printed in Great Britain by
Latimer Trend & Co Ltd Plymouth

Contents

THE EARTH-OWL   *page* 7

THE ADAPTABLE MOUNTAIN   9
    DUGONG

MOON-ROSES   11

MOON-CLOUD GRIPE   13

MOON-HORRORS   15

MUSIC ON THE MOON   17

MOON-NASTURTIUMS   19

THE ARMIES OF THE MOON   20

MOON-DOG-DAISIES   24

MOON-HOPS   25

CACTUS-SICKNESS   27

CRAB-GRASS   29

TREE-DISEASE   31

THE BURROW WOLF   33

MOON-TULIPS   34

FOXGLOVES   35

MOON-TRANSPORT   37

MOON-FREAKS   39

THE SNAIL OF THE MOON   40

MOON-CABBAGE   41

THE SILENT EYE   43

THE DRACULA VINE   44

A MOON MAN-HUNT   45

The Earth Owl

Far undergrounded,
Moon-miners dumbfounded
Hear the speed-whistle
Of this living missile
As he tears through the strata
Or splits apart a
Subterrene Gibraltar,
His wings do not falter
At deposits of iron—
He just screws a new eye on
The end of his skull
Which is shaped with great skill
As a terrible drill
That revolves on his neck—
His spine is the spindle,
His body the handle,
His wings are the thrust—
In a gunshot of dust
Sparks, splinters and all he
Bursts from the mine-wall,
Shrieking "Ek, Ek!"
And crashing straight on
Is instantly gone.

The Adaptable Mountain Dugong

The Mountain Dugong is a simply fantastic animal.
It lives mainly in extinct volcanoes, uttering its lonely call
Which nobody answers, because it is the sole Mountain
Dugong, there are no others at all.

It keeps alive with a number of surprising tricks.
It looks like a table, just as stick insects look like sticks.
So nobody interferes, they think it's an old table dumped
there by passing hicks.

But lo, what is under that most common-looking table?
Spare heads and legs in great assortment, all looking very
much alive and able.
The Mountain Dugong is its own Noah's Ark, and he will
not be stuck with any one label.

For instance, here comes a pack of wild dogs, each with a
mouth like a refuse bin.
They have smelt the Mountain Dugong's peculiar fried fish
smell and want to get their teeth in,
Because wild dogs need to devour every living thing in all
directions and to them this is no sin.

But the Mountain Dugong is already prepared, the wild dogs
cannot shock it.

He unscrews his table-legs and screws a greyhound leg into
    each socket
And is off over the crater-edge with all his equipment in three
    leaps like a rubber rocket.

The wild dogs begin to wear him down, they head him in a
    circle, they bring him to a stop, they gather in a ring,
But all this time the Mountain Dugong has not been malinger-
    ing.
He has screwed on to himself the headpiece of a tiger and in no
    time those wild dogs are a pile of chewed string.

This is how the adaptable Mountain Dugong carries on with-
    out loss.
He will screw on reindeer feet and head where there is nothing
    but Arctic moss.
Where there is nothing but sand the legs and hump of a camel
    soon get him across.

And he is forced to such tricks because there will never be
    another of his sort.
He has to keep himself in circulation by means no sane
    traveller would report.
I record his habits here, in case he should never again be seen
    or caught.

Moon-Roses

The moon's roses are very odd,
Each one the size of a turkey.
Over the fields they ponderously plod
Since their flight is dangerously jerky.

They lay eggs
With one long ear and three rabbity legs
And hatch them by pulling their
    spigots out like kegs.

Moon-Cloud Gripe

Moon-Cloud gripe first shows
By a whitening of the nose.
Then your hair begins to stir,
Your eyes begin to blur.
Then you go blue,
You shiver and say "Flu".
Then between your fingertips
A blue spark skips.
Then an amazing red
Zag zigs up from your head
And splits the ceiling.
You have the feeling
You are going to explode.
You are rumbling like a road
Under a ten-ton wagon.
Then a long orange dragon
Like a rip-saw tears
From your mouth and flares
The furniture to ash.
Down you crash.
The walls split and shake.
Neighbours shout "Earthquake!"
(How can they tell
It's just that you're not well?)

The only cure, they say,
Is to sigh for a whole day.

Moon-Horrors

When he has dined, the man-eating tiger leaves certain signs.
But nothing betrays the moon's hideous number nines.
Nobody knows where they sleep off their immense meals.
They strike so fatally nobody knows how one feels.
One-eyed, one-legged, they start out of the ground with
such a shout
The chosen victim's eyes instantly fall out.
They do not leave so much as a hair but smack their chops
And go off thinner than ever with grotesque hops.

Now the shark will take a snack by shearing off half a swimmer.
Over the moon presides a predator even grimmer.
Descending without warning from the interstellar heavens
Whirling like lathes, arrive the fearful horde of number
sevens.
Whatever they touch, whether owl or elephant, poet or
scientist,
The wretched victim wilts instantly to a puff of purple mist
And before he can utter a cry or say goodbye to kith and kin
Those thin-gut number sevens have sucked him ravenously in.

Mosquitoes seem dreadful, for they drink at a man as he sleeps.
Night and day over the moon a far craftier horror creeps.
It is hard to know what species of creature you would have
to be
To escape the attentions of the moon's horrible number three.

He attacks as a nightmare, and the sleeper dreams he is being
    turned inside out
And sucked dry like an orange, and when he wakes it has all
    come about.
Ever afterwards he is perfectly hollow and dry, while his
    precious insides
Nourish some gross number three wherever that monster
    now resides.

But the thing that specializes in hunting down the great hero
Is the flying strangler, the silent zero.
It is luckily quite rare, perhaps there is only one.
According to legend it lives sleepily coiled around the sun.
But when a moon-hero appears it descends and hovers just
    over his head.
His enemies call it a halo, but his friends see it and tremble
    with dread.
And sure enough, in the very best of his days,
That zero drops around his neck, tightens, and whirls away
    with him into the sun's blaze.

Music on the Moon

The pianos on the moon are so long
The pianist's hand must be fifteen fingers strong.

The violins on the moon are so violent
They have to be sunk in deep wells, and then they only seem
   to be silent.

The bassoons on the moon blow no notes
But huge blue loons that flap slowly away with undulating
   throats.

Now harmonicas on the moon are humourous,
The tunes produce German Measles, but the speckles more
   numerous.

Of a trumpet on the moon you can never hear enough
Because it puffs the trumpeter up like a balloon and he floats
   off.

Double basses on the moon are a risk all right,
At the first note enormous black hands appear and carry
   away everything in sight.

Even a triangle on the moon is risky,
One ping—and there's your head a half bottle of Irish
   whisky.

In the same way, be careful with the flute—
Because wherever he is, your father will find himself converted
    into a disgusting old boot.

On the whole it's best to stick to the moon's drums.
Whatever damage they do is so far off in space the news
    never comes.

Moon-Nasturtiums

Nasturtiums on earth are small and seething with horrible
    green caterpillars.
On the moon they are giant, jungles of them, and swarming
    with noisy gorillas.
And the green caterpillars there are the size of anacondas.
The butterflies that hatch from those are one of the moon's
    greatest wonders.
Though few survive the depredations of the gorillas
Who are partial to the succulent huge eggs that produce such
    caterpillars.

The Armies of the Moon

Many as the troubles upon the old moon are,
The worst is its unending Civil War.

The soldiers of the Moon-Dark are round and small.
Each clanks like a tank, blue armour covering all.
He wears asbestos overalls under his clatter.
So if he's thrown to the volcanoes it does not matter.
His weapon is a sackful of bloodsucking vampires
(Wars on the moon are without rules or umpires)
He flings these bats one at a time into the enemy host.
When it returns full he sends it to the first aid post
Where it gives up the blood for transfusions later in the
    battle.
Then it flies back to its owner with renewed mettle.

The soldiers of the Moon-Light are tall and thin.
They seem to be glisteningly naked, but are in fact silvered
    with tin.
They are defensive fighters, but pretty hot—
Their armament is an electric torch and a lobsterpot.
They flash their beam into the vampire's eyes and so puzzle
    it,
Then cram the lobsterpot on to its head, and so muzzle it.
They long for the last great battle in which they will catch
Every vampire the Moon-Darkers have been able to hatch.

Then they will rush upon the helpless Moon-Darkers and
  soon
With knitting-needles abolish them forever from the face of
  the moon.

Moon-Dog-Daisies

Dog-daisies on the moon run in packs
And it is their habit to carry moon-bees on their backs.
Dog-daisies live mainly on the small squealing sounders of
    sow-thistles
That charge about the moon's canyons, and the daisies are
    not deterrred by their bristles.
When a sow-thistle has given up the ghost to the daisy-dogs
Those moon-bees pounce down on to the feast and make
    themselves hogs.

Moon-Hops

Hops are a menace on the moon, a nuisance crop.
From hilltop to hilltop they hop hopelessly without stop.
Nobody knows what they want to find, they just go on till
    they drop,
Clip-clop at first, then flip-flop, then slip-slop, till finally they
    droopily drop and all their pods pop.

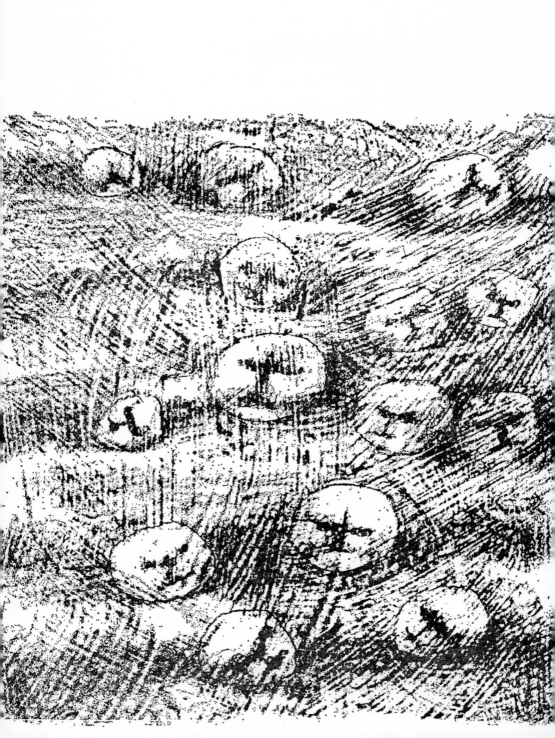

Cactus-Sickness

I hope you never contract
The lunar galloping cact-
-us, which is when dimples
Suddenly turn to pimples,
And these pimples bud—
Except for the odd dud—
Each one into a head with hair
And a face just like the one you wear.
These heads grow pea-size to begin
From your brows, your nose, your cheeks and your
      chin.
But soon enough they're melon-size,
All with mouths and shining eyes.
Within five days your poor neck spreads
A bunch of ten or fifteen heads
All hungry, arguing or singing
(Somewhere under your own head's ringing).
And so for one whole tedious week
You must admit you are a freak.

And then, perhaps when you gently cough
For silence, one of the heads drops off.
Their uproar instantly comes to a stop.
Then in silence, plop by plop,
With eyes and mouth most firmly closed,
Your rival heads, in turn deposed,

Land like pumpkins round your feet.
You walk on feeling light and neat.

In the next mirror are assured
That now you stand completely cured.

Crab-Grass

When you get to the moon, watch out for crab-grass.
It is in complete control of the moon's badlands, alas.

It drives the foolish gooseberries in fat gaggling flocks
Over high cliffs so that they split and lie helplessly edible
    below on the rocks.

It herds the Moon-Potatoes through their great seas of
    Volcanic ash
And nips their flippers so they leap ashore and flounder where
    they cannot so much as splash.

When a crab-grass comes upon a benighted tourist,
Of five hundred possible ends he may meet, that is the surest.

A crab-grass is ginger and hairy, and usually moves about six
    inches per year
In hordes of up to ten million, but that is its bottom gear.

You know a crab-grass is about to attack, by its excited hoot.
It has no eyes, so do not wait to see the whites of those before
    you shoot.

Tree-Disease

On the moon with great ease
You can catch tree-disease.
The symptoms are birds
Seeming interested in your words
And examining your ears.
Then a root peers
From under the nail
Of your big toe, then
You'd better get cured quick
Or you'll be really sick.

The Burrow Wolf

A kind of wolf lives in the moon's holes
Waiting for meteorites to score goals.

The meteorites come down blazing with velocity
And this wolf greets them with a huge grin of ferocity.

Whack to the back of his gullet go those glowing rocks
And the wolf's eyes start clean out of his head on eleven
    inch stalks.

But only for a moment, then he smiles and swallows
And shuts his eyes as over the melt of marshmallows.

Rockets nosediving on to the moon for modern adventures
Will have to reckon with those abnormal dentures.

Many a spaceman in the years to come
Will be pestled with meteorites in that horny tum.

If he does not dive direct into those jaws
He may well wander in there after a short pause.

For over the moon general madness reigns—
Bad when the light waxes, worse when it wanes—

And he might lunatically mistake this wolf for his wife.
So the man in the moon ended *his* life.

Moon-Tulips

Tulips on the moon are a kind of military band.

A bed of crimson ones will march up to your window and
take its stand.

Then out of their flashing brass and silver they rip some
Prussian fanfare.

Nobody asked them, and nobody takes any notice of their
blare.

After a while, they about turn and to kettledrums goose-step
away.

Soon under somebody else's window they are presenting the
same deafening bouquet.

Foxgloves

Foxgloves on the moon keep to dark caves.
They come out at the dark of the moon only and in waves
Swarm through the moon-towns and wherever there's a
    chink
Slip into the houses and spill all the money, clink-clink,
And crumple the notes and re-arrange the silver dishes,
And dip hands into the goldfish bowls and stir the goldfishes,
And thumb the edges of mirrors, and touch the sleepers
Then at once vanish into the far distance with a wild laugh
    leaving the house smelling faintly of Virginia Creepers.

Moon-Transport

Some people on the moon are so idle
They will not so much as saunter, much less sidle.

But if they cannot bear to walk, or try,
How do they get to the places where they lie?

They gather together, as people do for a bus.
"All aboard, whoever's coming with us."

Then they climb on to each other till they are all
Clinging in one enormous human ball.

Then they roll, and so, without lifting their feet,
Progress quite successfully down the street.

Moon-Freaks

The half-man is a frequent freak,
  One ear, one eye, and so on.
He cannot turn the other cheek
  And has only one foot to go slow on.
    He can't ride a bicycle or hobby-horse.
    He does everything single-handed of course.

Another sort of people look like a sort of pale spider.
They are actually nothing but huge human hands.
They gallop round on four fingers and the thumb sits up
  as a rider.

Another sort of people are condemned to being just feet,
Wandering about without ankles or knees or thighs.
They can't shake hands so they just kick when they meet.
They are great runners but since they have no eyes
Are constantly tripping on stones and charging into walls,
But they are so low they never get hurt in their falls.
A strange thing—if one stops, all the rest line up behind
  in a queue.
Otherwise they are quite useless and have nothing to do.

The moon's book-people simply love to read.
When they feel like reading, all they need
Is to meet with a friend. And thereupon
Each holds the other open and reads on.

39

The Snail of the Moon

Saddest of all things on the moon is the snail without a shell.
You locate him by his wail, a wail heart-rending and terrible

Which sounds as though some thing had punctured him.
His battle for progress is both slow and grim.

He is sad, wet and cold, like a huge tear
In a thin skin. He wanders far and near

Searching for a shelter from the sun—
For the first sun-beam will melt and make him run.

So moving in moon-dark only he must keep going,
With muscles rippling and saliva flowing,

But nowhere on the moon is there garage
For such a snail. He is not merely large

He is over a mile from side to side.
It's useless him seeking any place to hide.

So wailingly and craning his periscopes
Over the dark bulge of the moon he gropes.

He has searched every inch of the moon. I guess
That silver is snail-saliva silveriness.

Moon-Cabbage

Cabbages on the moon are not cabbages.
They are little old women, gabbing old baggages.

Where our cabbages are bundles of leaves, gently flip-flapping
Those are bundles of great loose lips, yappity-yap-yapping.

Yappity-yap, yappity-yap, yappity-yap-yap-yap!
Where our cabbages have hearts, those have gossip gushing
    out of a gap.

Not all of them are just bundles of lips. It appears
Some are in fact bundles of flapping ears, just like bundles of
    small elephant ears.

Flappity-flap, flappity-flap, flappity-flap-flap-flap!
Our cabbages are worn out by caterpillars, but those get
    ragged on sheer yap.

So some are all yap and some are all ears and their mutual
    amusements resound.
And they are so tough they can go on at that till their one
    scaly old shank grows right down into the ground.

The Silent Eye

On the moon lives an eye.
It flies about in the sky,
Staring, glaring, or just peering.
You can't see what it uses for steering.
It is about the size of a large owl,
But has no feathers, and so is by no means a fowl.
Sometimes it zips overhead from horizon to horizon
Then you know it has seen something surprisin'.
Mostly it hovers just above you and stares
Rudely down into your most private affairs.
Nobody minds it much, they say it has charm.
It has no mouth or hands, so how could it do harm?
Besides, as I say, it has these appealing ways.
When you are sitting sadly under crushing dismays,
This eye floats up and gazes at you like a mourner,
Then droops and wilts and a huge tear sags from its corner,
And soon it is sobbing and expressing such woe
You begin to wish it would stop it and just go.

The Dracula Vine

People on the moon love a pet.
But there's only one pet you can get—
The Dracula Vine, a monstrous sight!
But the moon-people like it all right.

This pet looks like a climbing plant
Made from parts of elephant.
But each flower is a hippo's head
Endlessly gaping to be fed.

Now this pet eats everything—
Whatever you can shovel or fling.
It snaps up all your old cardboard boxes
Your empty cans and your stuffed foxes.

And wonder of wonders! The very flower
You have given something to devour
Sprouts on the spot a luscious kind of pear
Without pips, and you can eat it there.

So this is a useful pet
And loyal if well-treat.
But if you treat it badly
It will wander off sadly

Till somebody with more garbage than you
Gives its flowers something to do.

A Moon Man-Hunt

A man-hunt on the moon is full of horrible sights and sounds.
There are these foxes in red jackets, they are their own horses
 and hounds.
They have unhuman eyes, O they are savage out of all bounds.

They swagger at the meet, their grins going back under their
 ears.
They are sociable to begin with, showing each other their
 long fangs and their no fears.
They pretend it is all a good game and nothing to do with
 death and its introductory tears.

Now one yip! and they are off, tails waving in sinister accord.
To tell the truth, they are a murderous depraved-looking
 horde.
Sniff sniff! they come over the acres, till some strolling squire
 looks up and sees them pattering toward.

The sweat jumps on his brow freezingly and the hair stands
 on his thighs.
His lips writhe, his tongue fluffs dry as a duster, tears pour
 from his eyes.
His bowels twist like a strong snake, and for some seconds he
 sways there useless with terrified surprise.

"Ha Ha!" go all the foxes in unison.

"That menace, that noble rural vermin, the gentry, there's
    one!"
The dirt flies from their paws and the squire begins hopelessly
    to run.

But what chance does that wretch have against such an animal?
Five catch his heels, and one on his nose, and ten on each arm,
    he goes down with a yell.
It is terrible, it is terrible, O it is terrible!